This Recipe Book Belongs to...

_____

_____

M.DERN
STUDIO

Copyright © M.DERN STUDIO. All rights reserved. No part of this publication may be reproduced, stored in a retrieval system, or transmitted in any form or by any means, electronic, mechanical, photocopying, recording, or otherwise, without written permission of the publisher.

Contents

1.
2.
3.
4.
5.
6.
7.
8.
9.
10.
11.
12.
13.
14.
15.
16.
17.
18.
19.
20.
21.
22.
23.
24.
25.

Contents

26.	
27.	
28.	
29.	
30.	
31.	
32.	
33.	
34.	
35.	
36.	
37.	
38.	
39.	
40.	
41.	
42.	
43.	
44.	
45.	
46.	
47.	
48.	
49.	
50.	

Contents

51.	
52.	
53.	
54.	
55.	
56.	
57.	
58.	
59.	
60.	
61.	
62.	
63.	
64.	
65.	
66.	
67.	
68.	
69.	
70.	
71.	
72.	
73.	
74.	
75.	

Contents

76.	
77.	
78.	
79.	
80.	
81.	
82.	
83.	
84.	
85.	
86.	
87.	
88.	
89.	
90.	
91.	
92.	
93.	
94.	
95.	
96.	
97.	
98.	
99.	
100.	

1

RECIPE:

DIFFICULTY:
☐☐☐☐☐

RATING:
♡♡♡♡♡

SERVES:

....

COOKING TEMP:

....

PREP TIME:

....

COOK TIME:

....

TOOLS:

....
....
....
....
....
....

INGREDIENTS:

DIRECTIONS:

RECIPE:

2

INGREDIENTS:

_____
_____
_____
_____
_____
_____
_____
_____
_____
_____

DIRECTIONS:

_____
_____
_____
_____
_____
_____
_____
_____
_____
_____
_____

DIFFICULTY:
☐ ☐ ☐ ☐ ☐

RATING:
♡ ♡ ♡ ♡ ♡

SERVES:
....

COOKING TEMP:
....

PREP TIME:
....

COOK TIME:
....

TOOLS:
....
....
....
....
....
....

3

RECIPE:

DIFFICULTY:
☐☐☐☐☐

RATING:
♡♡♡♡♡

SERVES:

COOKING TEMP:

PREP TIME:

COOK TIME:

TOOLS:

INGREDIENTS:

DIRECTIONS:

RECIPE:

4

INGREDIENTS:

_____
_____
_____
_____
_____
_____
_____
_____
_____
_____
_____
_____

DIRECTIONS:

_____
_____
_____
_____
_____
_____
_____
_____
_____
_____

DIFFICULTY:
☐ ☐ ☐ ☐ ☐

RATING:
♡ ♡ ♡ ♡ ♡

SERVES:
....

COOKING TEMP:
....

PREP TIME:
....

COOK TIME:
....

TOOLS:
....
....
....
....
....
....

5

RECIPE:

DIFFICULTY:
☐☐☐☐☐

RATING:
♡♡♡♡♡

SERVES:

COOKING TEMP:

PREP TIME:

COOK TIME:

TOOLS:

INGREDIENTS:

DIRECTIONS:

RECIPE:

6

INGREDIENTS:

DIRECTIONS:

DIFFICULTY:
☐☐☐☐☐

RATING:
♡♡♡♡♡

SERVES:

COOKING TEMP:

PREP TIME:

COOK TIME:

TOOLS:

7

RECIPE:

DIFFICULTY:
☐☐☐☐☐

RATING:
♡♡♡♡♡

SERVES:
....

COOKING TEMP:
....

PREP TIME:
....

COOK TIME:
....

TOOLS:
....
....
....
....
....

INGREDIENTS:

DIRECTIONS:

RECIPE:

8

INGREDIENTS:
_____
_____
_____
_____
_____
_____
_____
_____
_____
_____
_____

DIFFICULTY:
☐☐☐☐☐

RATING:
♡♡♡♡♡

SERVES:
....

COOKING TEMP:
....

DIRECTIONS:
_____
_____
_____
_____
_____
_____
_____
_____
_____
_____
_____
_____

PREP TIME:
....

COOK TIME:
....

TOOLS:
....
....
....
....
....
....

9

RECIPE:

DIFFICULTY:
☐☐☐☐☐

RATING:
♡♡♡♡♡

SERVES:
....

COOKING TEMP:
....

PREP TIME:
....

COOK TIME:
....

TOOLS:
....
....
....
....
....

INGREDIENTS:
_____
_____
_____
_____
_____
_____
_____
_____
_____
_____

DIRECTIONS:
_____
_____
_____
_____
_____
_____
_____
_____
_____
_____
_____
_____

RECIPE:

10

INGREDIENTS:
_____
_____
_____
_____
_____
_____
_____
_____
_____
_____

DIRECTIONS:
_____
_____
_____
_____
_____
_____
_____
_____
_____
_____
_____

DIFFICULTY:
☐☐☐☐☐

RATING:
♡♡♡♡♡

SERVES:
....

COOKING TEMP:
....

PREP TIME:
....

COOK TIME:
....

TOOLS:
....
....
....
....
....
....

11

RECIPE:

DIFFICULTY:
☐☐☐☐☐

RATING:
♡♡♡♡♡

SERVES:

COOKING TEMP:

PREP TIME:

COOK TIME:

TOOLS:

INGREDIENTS:

DIRECTIONS:

RECIPE:

12

INGREDIENTS:

_____
_____
_____
_____
_____
_____
_____
_____
_____
_____
_____

DIRECTIONS:

_____
_____
_____
_____
_____
_____
_____
_____
_____
_____
_____
_____
_____

DIFFICULTY:
☐ ☐ ☐ ☐ ☐

RATING:
♡ ♡ ♡ ♡ ♡

SERVES:
....

COOKING TEMP:
....

PREP TIME:
....

COOK TIME:
....

TOOLS:
....
....
....
....
....
....

13

RECIPE:

DIFFICULTY:
☐☐☐☐☐

RATING:
♡♡♡♡♡

SERVES:
....

COOKING TEMP:
....

PREP TIME:
....

COOK TIME:
....

TOOLS:
....
....
....
....
....

INGREDIENTS:
_____
_____
_____
_____
_____
_____
_____
_____
_____

DIRECTIONS:
_____
_____
_____
_____
_____
_____
_____
_____
_____
_____
_____
_____

RECIPE:

14

INGREDIENTS:
_____
_____
_____
_____
_____
_____
_____
_____
_____
_____
_____
_____

DIRECTIONS:
_____
_____
_____
_____
_____
_____
_____
_____
_____
_____
_____
_____
_____
_____

DIFFICULTY:
☐ ☐ ☐ ☐ ☐

RATING:
♡ ♡ ♡ ♡ ♡

SERVES:
....

COOKING TEMP:
....

PREP TIME:
....

COOK TIME:
....

TOOLS:
....
....
....
....
....
....

15

RECIPE:

DIFFICULTY:
☐☐☐☐☐

RATING:
♡♡♡♡♡

SERVES:

COOKING TEMP:

PREP TIME:

COOK TIME:

TOOLS:

INGREDIENTS:

DIRECTIONS:

16

RECIPE:

INGREDIENTS:

_____
_____
_____
_____
_____
_____
_____
_____
_____

DIRECTIONS:

_____
_____
_____
_____
_____
_____
_____
_____
_____

DIFFICULTY:
☐☐☐☐☐

RATING:
♡♡♡♡♡

SERVES:
....

COOKING TEMP:
....

PREP TIME:
....

COOK TIME:
....

TOOLS:
....
....
....
....
....
....

17

RECIPE:

DIFFICULTY:
☐☐☐☐☐

RATING:
♡♡♡♡♡

SERVES:

COOKING TEMP:

PREP TIME:

COOK TIME:

TOOLS:

INGREDIENTS:

DIRECTIONS:

RECIPE:

18

INGREDIENTS:

DIRECTIONS:

DIFFICULTY:
☐ ☐ ☐ ☐ ☐

RATING:
♡ ♡ ♡ ♡ ♡

SERVES:

....

COOKING TEMP:

....

PREP TIME:

....

COOK TIME:

....

TOOLS:

....
....
....
....
....
....

19

RECIPE:

DIFFICULTY:
☐☐☐☐☐

RATING:
♡♡♡♡♡

SERVES:

COOKING TEMP:

PREP TIME:

COOK TIME:

TOOLS:

INGREDIENTS:

DIRECTIONS:

RECIPE:

20

INGREDIENTS:
_____
_____
_____
_____
_____
_____
_____
_____
_____
_____
_____

DIFFICULTY:
☐☐☐☐☐

RATING:
♡♡♡♡♡

SERVES:
....

COOKING TEMP:
....

DIRECTIONS:
_____
_____
_____
_____
_____
_____
_____
_____
_____
_____
_____
_____
_____
_____
_____

PREP TIME:
....

COOK TIME:
....

TOOLS:
....
....
....
....
....

21

RECIPE:

DIFFICULTY:
☐☐☐☐☐

RATING:
♡♡♡♡♡

SERVES:
....

COOKING TEMP:
....

PREP TIME:
....

COOK TIME:
....

TOOLS:
....
....
....
....
....

INGREDIENTS:

DIRECTIONS:

RECIPE:

22

INGREDIENTS:

_____
_____
_____
_____
_____
_____
_____
_____
_____
_____

DIRECTIONS:

_____
_____
_____
_____
_____
_____
_____
_____
_____
_____

DIFFICULTY:
☐☐☐☐☐

RATING:
♡♡♡♡♡

SERVES:
....

COOKING TEMP:
....

PREP TIME:
....

COOK TIME:
....

TOOLS:
....
....
....
....
....
....

23

RECIPE:

DIFFICULTY:

RATING:
♡♡♡♡♡

SERVES:
....

COOKING TEMP:
....

PREP TIME:
....

COOK TIME:
....

TOOLS:
....
....
....
....

INGREDIENTS:

DIRECTIONS:

RECIPE:

24

INGREDIENTS:

_____

DIRECTIONS:

_____

DIFFICULTY:
☐ ☐ ☐ ☐ ☐

RATING:
♡ ♡ ♡ ♡ ♡

SERVES:
....

COOKING TEMP:
....

PREP TIME:
....

COOK TIME:
....

TOOLS:
....

25

RECIPE:

DIFFICULTY:
☐ ☐ ☐ ☐ ☐

RATING:
♡ ♡ ♡ ♡ ♡

SERVES:

COOKING TEMP:

PREP TIME:

COOK TIME:

TOOLS:

INGREDIENTS:

DIRECTIONS:

RECIPE:

26

INGREDIENTS:
_____
_____
_____
_____
_____
_____
_____
_____
_____
_____

DIRECTIONS:
_____
_____
_____
_____
_____
_____
_____
_____
_____
_____
_____
_____
_____
_____

DIFFICULTY:
☐☐☐☐☐

RATING:
♡♡♡♡♡

SERVES:
....

COOKING TEMP:
....

PREP TIME:
....

COOK TIME:
....

TOOLS:
....
....
....
....
....
....

27

RECIPE:

DIFFICULTY:
☐☐☐☐☐

RATING:
♡♡♡♡♡

SERVES:

COOKING TEMP:

PREP TIME:

COOK TIME:

TOOLS:

INGREDIENTS:

DIRECTIONS:

RECIPE:

28

INGREDIENTS:
_____
_____
_____
_____
_____
_____
_____
_____
_____
_____

DIRECTIONS:
_____
_____
_____
_____
_____
_____
_____
_____
_____
_____

DIFFICULTY:
☐☐☐☐☐

RATING:
♡♡♡♡♡

SERVES:
....

COOKING TEMP:
....

PREP TIME:
....

COOK TIME:
....

TOOLS:
....
....
....
....
....
....

29

RECIPE:

DIFFICULTY:
☐☐☐☐☐

RATING:
♡♡♡♡♡

SERVES:
....

COOKING TEMP:
....

PREP TIME:
....

COOK TIME:
....

TOOLS:
....
....
....
....

INGREDIENTS:
_____
_____
_____
_____
_____
_____
_____
_____

DIRECTIONS:
_____
_____
_____
_____
_____
_____
_____
_____
_____
_____
_____

RECIPE:

30

INGREDIENTS:

_____
_____
_____
_____
_____
_____
_____
_____
_____
_____
_____
_____

DIRECTIONS:

_____
_____
_____
_____
_____
_____
_____
_____
_____
_____
_____
_____
_____
_____
_____

DIFFICULTY:
☐ ☐ ☐ ☐ ☐

RATING:
♡ ♡ ♡ ♡ ♡

SERVES:
....

COOKING TEMP:
....

PREP TIME:
....

COOK TIME:
....

TOOLS:
....
....
....
....
....

31

RECIPE:

DIFFICULTY:
☐☐☐☐☐

RATING:
♡♡♡♡♡

SERVES:

COOKING TEMP:

PREP TIME:

COOK TIME:

TOOLS:

INGREDIENTS:

DIRECTIONS:

RECIPE:

32

INGREDIENTS:

DIFFICULTY:
☐☐☐☐☐

RATING:
♡♡♡♡♡

SERVES:

COOKING TEMP:

DIRECTIONS:

PREP TIME:

COOK TIME:

TOOLS:

33

RECIPE:

DIFFICULTY:
☐☐☐☐☐

RATING:
♡♡♡♡♡

SERVES:

COOKING TEMP:

PREP TIME:

COOK TIME:

TOOLS:

INGREDIENTS:

DIRECTIONS:

RECIPE:

34

INGREDIENTS:

_____
_____
_____
_____
_____
_____
_____
_____
_____
_____
_____
_____

DIRECTIONS:

_____
_____
_____
_____
_____
_____
_____
_____
_____
_____
_____
_____
_____

DIFFICULTY:
☐ ☐ ☐ ☐ ☐

RATING:
♡ ♡ ♡ ♡ ♡

SERVES:
....

COOKING TEMP:
....

PREP TIME:
....

COOK TIME:
....

TOOLS:
....
....
....
....
....
....

35

RECIPE:

DIFFICULTY:
☐☐☐☐☐

RATING:
♡♡♡♡♡

SERVES:

COOKING TEMP:

PREP TIME:

COOK TIME:

TOOLS:

INGREDIENTS:

DIRECTIONS:

RECIPE:

36

INGREDIENTS:

_____

_____

_____

_____

_____

_____

_____

_____

_____

_____

_____

_____

DIRECTIONS:

_____

_____

_____

_____

_____

_____

_____

_____

_____

_____

_____

_____

_____

_____

DIFFICULTY:
☐ ☐ ☐ ☐ ☐

RATING:
♡ ♡ ♡ ♡ ♡

SERVES:
....

COOKING TEMP:
....

PREP TIME:
....

COOK TIME:
....

TOOLS:
....
....
....
....
....
....

37

RECIPE:

DIFFICULTY:
☐☐☐☐☐

RATING:
♡♡♡♡♡

SERVES:
....

COOKING TEMP:
....

PREP TIME:
....

COOK TIME:
....

TOOLS:
....
....
....
....
....
....

INGREDIENTS:

DIRECTIONS:

RECIPE:

38

INGREDIENTS:

DIFFICULTY:
☐☐☐☐☐

RATING:
♡♡♡♡♡

SERVES:

COOKING TEMP:

DIRECTIONS:

PREP TIME:

COOK TIME:

TOOLS:

39

RECIPE:

DIFFICULTY:
☐☐☐☐☐

RATING:
♡♡♡♡♡

SERVES:

COOKING TEMP:

PREP TIME:

COOK TIME:

TOOLS:

INGREDIENTS:

DIRECTIONS:

RECIPE:

INGREDIENTS:
_____
_____
_____
_____
_____
_____
_____
_____
_____

DIFFICULTY:
☐☐☐☐☐

RATING:
♡♡♡♡♡

SERVES:
....

COOKING TEMP:
....

DIRECTIONS:
_____
_____
_____
_____
_____
_____
_____
_____
_____
_____

PREP TIME:
....

COOK TIME:
....

TOOLS:
....
....
....
....
....
....

41

RECIPE:

DIFFICULTY:
☐☐☐☐☐

RATING:
♡♡♡♡♡

SERVES:

COOKING TEMP:

PREP TIME:

COOK TIME:

TOOLS:

INGREDIENTS:

DIRECTIONS:

RECIPE:

42

INGREDIENTS:

_____
_____
_____
_____
_____
_____
_____
_____
_____
_____
_____

DIRECTIONS:

_____
_____
_____
_____
_____
_____
_____
_____
_____
_____
_____
_____
_____

DIFFICULTY:
☐ ☐ ☐ ☐ ☐

RATING:
♡ ♡ ♡ ♡ ♡

SERVES:
....

COOKING TEMP:
....

PREP TIME:
....

COOK TIME:
....

TOOLS:
....
....
....
....
....
....

43

RECIPE:

DIFFICULTY:
☐☐☐☐☐

RATING:
♡♡♡♡♡

SERVES:

COOKING TEMP:

PREP TIME:

COOK TIME:

TOOLS:

INGREDIENTS:

DIRECTIONS:

RECIPE:

44

INGREDIENTS:

DIFFICULTY:

RATING:
♡♡♡♡♡

SERVES:

COOKING TEMP:

PREP TIME:

DIRECTIONS:

COOK TIME:

TOOLS:

45

RECIPE:

DIFFICULTY:
☐☐☐☐☐

RATING:
♡♡♡♡♡

SERVES:

COOKING TEMP:

PREP TIME:

COOK TIME:

TOOLS:

INGREDIENTS:

DIRECTIONS:

RECIPE:

INGREDIENTS:

DIFFICULTY:

RATING:

SERVES:

COOKING TEMP:

DIRECTIONS:

PREP TIME:

COOK TIME:

TOOLS:

47

RECIPE:

DIFFICULTY:
☐☐☐☐☐

RATING:
♡♡♡♡♡

SERVES:

COOKING TEMP:

PREP TIME:

COOK TIME:

TOOLS:

INGREDIENTS:

DIRECTIONS:

RECIPE:

48

INGREDIENTS:
_____
_____
_____
_____
_____
_____
_____
_____
_____
_____
_____
_____

DIRECTIONS:
_____
_____
_____
_____
_____
_____
_____
_____
_____
_____
_____
_____
_____
_____

DIFFICULTY:
☐☐☐☐☐

RATING:
♡♡♡♡♡

SERVES:
....

COOKING TEMP:
....

PREP TIME:
....

COOK TIME:
....

TOOLS:
....
....
....
....
....
....

49

RECIPE:

DIFFICULTY:
☐☐☐☐☐

RATING:
♡♡♡♡♡

SERVES:

COOKING TEMP:

PREP TIME:

COOK TIME:

TOOLS:

INGREDIENTS:

DIRECTIONS:

RECIPE:

50

INGREDIENTS:

DIFFICULTY:
☐☐☐☐☐

RATING:
♡♡♡♡♡

SERVES:

....

COOKING TEMP:

....

DIRECTIONS:

PREP TIME:

....

COOK TIME:

....

TOOLS:

....
....
....
....
....
....

51

RECIPE:

DIFFICULTY:
☐ ☐ ☐ ☐ ☐

RATING:
♡ ♡ ♡ ♡ ♡

SERVES:

COOKING TEMP:

PREP TIME:

COOK TIME:

TOOLS:

INGREDIENTS:

DIRECTIONS:

RECIPE:

52

INGREDIENTS:

_____
_____
_____
_____
_____
_____
_____
_____
_____
_____

DIFFICULTY:
☐☐☐☐☐

RATING:
♡♡♡♡♡

SERVES:
....

COOKING TEMP:
....

DIRECTIONS:

_____
_____
_____
_____
_____
_____
_____
_____
_____
_____
_____
_____

PREP TIME:
....

COOK TIME:
....

TOOLS:
....
....
....
....
....
....

53

RECIPE:

DIFFICULTY:
☐☐☐☐☐

RATING:
♡♡♡♡♡

SERVES:
....

COOKING TEMP:
....

PREP TIME:
....

COOK TIME:
....

TOOLS:
....
....
....
....
....

INGREDIENTS:
_____
_____
_____
_____
_____
_____
_____
_____

DIRECTIONS:
_____
_____
_____
_____
_____
_____
_____
_____
_____
_____

RECIPE:

54

INGREDIENTS:

_____
_____
_____
_____
_____
_____
_____
_____
_____
_____
_____

DIRECTIONS:

_____
_____
_____
_____
_____
_____
_____
_____
_____
_____
_____
_____
_____
_____

DIFFICULTY:
☐ ☐ ☐ ☐ ☐

RATING:
♡ ♡ ♡ ♡ ♡

SERVES:
....

COOKING TEMP:
....

PREP TIME:
....

COOK TIME:
....

TOOLS:
....
....
....
....
....
....

# 55

RECIPE:

DIFFICULTY:
☐☐☐☐☐

RATING:
♡♡♡♡♡

SERVES:

COOKING TEMP:

PREP TIME:

COOK TIME:

TOOLS:

INGREDIENTS:

DIRECTIONS:

RECIPE:

56

INGREDIENTS:

_____
_____
_____
_____
_____
_____
_____
_____
_____
_____

DIFFICULTY:
☐☐☐☐☐

RATING:
♡♡♡♡♡

SERVES:
....

COOKING TEMP:
....

DIRECTIONS:

_____
_____
_____
_____
_____
_____
_____
_____
_____
_____
_____

PREP TIME:
....

COOK TIME:
....

TOOLS:
....
....
....
....
....
....

57

RECIPE:

DIFFICULTY:
☐☐☐☐☐

RATING:
♡♡♡♡♡

SERVES:

COOKING TEMP:

PREP TIME:

COOK TIME:

TOOLS:

INGREDIENTS:

DIRECTIONS:

RECIPE:

58

INGREDIENTS:

DIFFICULTY:

RATING:
♡♡♡♡♡

SERVES:

COOKING TEMP:

DIRECTIONS:

PREP TIME:

COOK TIME:

TOOLS:

59

RECIPE:

DIFFICULTY:
☐☐☐☐☐

RATING:
♡♡♡♡♡

SERVES:
....

COOKING TEMP:
....

PREP TIME:
....

COOK TIME:
....

TOOLS:
....
....
....
....
....

INGREDIENTS:
_____
_____
_____
_____
_____
_____
_____
_____

DIRECTIONS:
_____
_____
_____
_____
_____
_____
_____
_____
_____
_____
_____

RECIPE:

INGREDIENTS:

DIFFICULTY:
☐ ☐ ☐ ☐ ☐

RATING:
♡ ♡ ♡ ♡ ♡

SERVES:
....

COOKING TEMP:
....

DIRECTIONS:

PREP TIME:
....

COOK TIME:
....

TOOLS:
....
....
....
....
....
....

61

RECIPE:

DIFFICULTY:
☐ ☐ ☐ ☐ ☐

RATING:
♡ ♡ ♡ ♡ ♡

SERVES:

....

COOKING TEMP:

....

PREP TIME:

....

COOK TIME:

....

TOOLS:

....
....
....
....
....

INGREDIENTS:

DIRECTIONS:

RECIPE:

INGREDIENTS:
_____
_____
_____
_____
_____
_____
_____
_____
_____
_____
_____

DIFFICULTY:
☐☐☐☐☐

RATING:
♡♡♡♡♡

SERVES:
....

COOKING TEMP:
....

DIRECTIONS:
_____
_____
_____
_____
_____
_____
_____
_____
_____
_____
_____
_____

PREP TIME:
....

COOK TIME:
....

TOOLS:
....
....
....
....
....
....

63

RECIPE:

DIFFICULTY:
☐☐☐☐☐

RATING:
♡♡♡♡♡

SERVES:
....

COOKING TEMP:
....

PREP TIME:
....

COOK TIME:
....

TOOLS:
....
....
....
....
....

INGREDIENTS:
_____
_____
_____
_____
_____
_____
_____
_____
_____

DIRECTIONS:
_____
_____
_____
_____
_____
_____
_____
_____
_____
_____

RECIPE:

64

INGREDIENTS:

DIFFICULTY:
☐☐☐☐☐

RATING:
♡♡♡♡♡

SERVES:

....

COOKING TEMP:

....

DIRECTIONS:

PREP TIME:

....

COOK TIME:

....

TOOLS:

....
....
....
....
....
....

65

RECIPE:

DIFFICULTY:
☐☐☐☐☐

RATING:
♡♡♡♡♡

SERVES:

COOKING TEMP:

PREP TIME:

COOK TIME:

TOOLS:

INGREDIENTS:

DIRECTIONS:

RECIPE:

66

INGREDIENTS:

_____
_____
_____
_____
_____
_____
_____
_____
_____
_____
_____

DIFFICULTY:
☐ ☐ ☐ ☐ ☐

RATING:
♡ ♡ ♡ ♡ ♡

SERVES:
....

COOKING TEMP:
....

DIRECTIONS:

_____
_____
_____
_____
_____
_____
_____
_____
_____
_____
_____
_____
_____
_____
_____

PREP TIME:
....

COOK TIME:
....

TOOLS:
....
....
....
....
....
....

67

RECIPE:

DIFFICULTY:
☐ ☐ ☐ ☐ ☐

RATING:
♡ ♡ ♡ ♡ ♡

SERVES:

COOKING TEMP:

PREP TIME:

COOK TIME:

TOOLS:

INGREDIENTS:

DIRECTIONS:

RECIPE:

INGREDIENTS:
_____
_____
_____
_____
_____
_____
_____
_____
_____
_____
_____

DIRECTIONS:
_____
_____
_____
_____
_____
_____
_____
_____
_____
_____
_____
_____
_____

DIFFICULTY:
☐☐☐☐☐

RATING:
♡♡♡♡♡

SERVES:
....

COOKING TEMP:
....

PREP TIME:
....

COOK TIME:
....

TOOLS:
....
....
....
....
....
....

69

RECIPE:

DIFFICULTY:
☐☐☐☐☐

RATING:
♡♡♡♡♡

SERVES:
....

COOKING TEMP:
....

PREP TIME:
....

COOK TIME:
....

TOOLS:
....
....
....
....
....

INGREDIENTS:

DIRECTIONS:

RECIPE:

70

INGREDIENTS:

_____
_____
_____
_____
_____
_____
_____
_____
_____

DIRECTIONS:

_____
_____
_____
_____
_____
_____
_____
_____
_____
_____
_____

DIFFICULTY:
☐☐☐☐☐

RATING:
♡♡♡♡♡

SERVES:

....

COOKING TEMP:

....

PREP TIME:

....

COOK TIME:

....

TOOLS:

....
....
....
....
....
....

71

RECIPE:

DIFFICULTY:
☐☐☐☐☐

RATING:
♡♡♡♡♡

SERVES:

COOKING TEMP:

PREP TIME:

COOK TIME:

TOOLS:

INGREDIENTS:

DIRECTIONS:

RECIPE:

72

INGREDIENTS:

DIRECTIONS:

DIFFICULTY:
☐☐☐☐☐

RATING:
♡♡♡♡♡

SERVES:

COOKING TEMP:

PREP TIME:

COOK TIME:

TOOLS:

73

RECIPE:

DIFFICULTY:
☐☐☐☐☐

RATING:
♡♡♡♡♡

SERVES:
....

COOKING TEMP:
....

PREP TIME:
....

COOK TIME:
....

TOOLS:
....
....
....
....
....

INGREDIENTS:

DIRECTIONS:

RECIPE:

74

INGREDIENTS:
_____
_____
_____
_____
_____
_____
_____
_____
_____
_____
_____

DIFFICULTY:
☐☐☐☐☐

RATING:
♡♡♡♡♡

SERVES:
....

COOKING TEMP:
....

DIRECTIONS:
_____
_____
_____
_____
_____
_____
_____
_____
_____
_____
_____
_____
_____

PREP TIME:
....

COOK TIME:
....

TOOLS:
....
....
....
....
....
....

75

RECIPE:

DIFFICULTY:
☐ ☐ ☐ ☐ ☐

RATING:
♡ ♡ ♡ ♡ ♡

SERVES:
....

COOKING TEMP:
....

PREP TIME:
....

COOK TIME:
....

TOOLS:
....
....
....
....
....

INGREDIENTS:

DIRECTIONS:

RECIPE:

INGREDIENTS:
_____
_____
_____
_____
_____
_____
_____
_____

DIFFICULTY:
☐☐☐☐☐

RATING:
♡♡♡♡♡

SERVES:
....

COOKING TEMP:
....

DIRECTIONS:
_____
_____
_____
_____
_____
_____
_____
_____
_____
_____
_____
_____

PREP TIME:
....

COOK TIME:
....

TOOLS:
....
....
....
....
....
....

77

RECIPE:

DIFFICULTY:
☐☐☐☐☐

RATING:
♡♡♡♡♡

SERVES:
....

COOKING TEMP:
....

PREP TIME:
....

COOK TIME:
....

TOOLS:
....
....
....
....
....

INGREDIENTS:

DIRECTIONS:

RECIPE:

78

INGREDIENTS:

DIRECTIONS:

DIFFICULTY:
☐☐☐☐☐

RATING:
♡♡♡♡♡

SERVES:

COOKING TEMP:

PREP TIME:

COOK TIME:

TOOLS:

79

RECIPE:

DIFFICULTY:
☐☐☐☐☐

RATING:
♡♡♡♡♡

SERVES:

COOKING TEMP:

PREP TIME:

COOK TIME:

TOOLS:

INGREDIENTS:

DIRECTIONS:

RECIPE:

INGREDIENTS:
_____
_____
_____
_____
_____
_____
_____
_____
_____
_____

DIRECTIONS:
_____
_____
_____
_____
_____
_____
_____
_____
_____
_____
_____

DIFFICULTY:
☐☐☐☐☐

RATING:
♡♡♡♡♡

SERVES:
....

COOKING TEMP:
....

PREP TIME:
....

COOK TIME:
....

TOOLS:
....
....
....
....
....
....

81

RECIPE:

DIFFICULTY:
☐☐☐☐☐

RATING:
♡♡♡♡♡

SERVES:

COOKING TEMP:

PREP TIME:

COOK TIME:

TOOLS:

INGREDIENTS:

DIRECTIONS:

RECIPE:

INGREDIENTS:

DIFFICULTY:

RATING:

SERVES:

COOKING TEMP:

DIRECTIONS:

PREP TIME:

COOK TIME:

TOOLS:

83

RECIPE:

DIFFICULTY:
☐☐☐☐☐

RATING:
♡♡♡♡♡

SERVES:
....

COOKING TEMP:
....

PREP TIME:
....

COOK TIME:
....

TOOLS:
....
....
....
....
....

INGREDIENTS:

DIRECTIONS:

RECIPE:

84

INGREDIENTS:

DIFFICULTY:
☐☐☐☐☐

RATING:
♡♡♡♡♡

SERVES:

....

COOKING TEMP:

....

DIRECTIONS:

PREP TIME:

....

COOK TIME:

....

TOOLS:

....
....
....
....
....
....

85

RECIPE:

DIFFICULTY:
☐ ☐ ☐ ☐ ☐

RATING:
♡ ♡ ♡ ♡ ♡

SERVES:
....

COOKING TEMP:
....

PREP TIME:
....

COOK TIME:
....

TOOLS:
....
....
....
....
....

INGREDIENTS:

DIRECTIONS:

RECIPE:

86

INGREDIENTS:

DIFFICULTY:
☐☐☐☐☐

RATING:
♡♡♡♡♡

SERVES:

....

COOKING TEMP:

....

DIRECTIONS:

PREP TIME:

....

COOK TIME:

....

TOOLS:

....
....
....
....
....
....

87

RECIPE:

DIFFICULTY:
☐☐☐☐☐

RATING:
♡♡♡♡♡

SERVES:
....

COOKING TEMP:
....

PREP TIME:
....

COOK TIME:
....

TOOLS:
....
....
....
....
....

INGREDIENTS:

DIRECTIONS:

RECIPE:

88

INGREDIENTS:

_____
_____
_____
_____
_____
_____
_____
_____
_____
_____

DIRECTIONS:

_____
_____
_____
_____
_____
_____
_____
_____
_____
_____
_____
_____

DIFFICULTY:
☐☐☐☐☐

RATING:
♡♡♡♡♡

SERVES:
....

COOKING TEMP:
....

PREP TIME:
....

COOK TIME:
....

TOOLS:
....
....
....
....
....
....

89

RECIPE:

DIFFICULTY:
☐☐☐☐☐

RATING:
♡♡♡♡♡

SERVES:

COOKING TEMP:

PREP TIME:

COOK TIME:

TOOLS:

INGREDIENTS:

DIRECTIONS:

RECIPE:

90

INGREDIENTS:

DIFFICULTY:
☐☐☐☐☐

RATING:
♡♡♡♡♡

SERVES:
....

COOKING TEMP:
....

DIRECTIONS:

PREP TIME:
....

COOK TIME:
....

TOOLS:
....
....
....
....
....
....

91

RECIPE:

DIFFICULTY:
☐☐☐☐☐

RATING:
♡♡♡♡♡

SERVES:
....

COOKING TEMP:
....

PREP TIME:
....

COOK TIME:
....

TOOLS:
....
....
....
....
....
....

INGREDIENTS:
_____
_____
_____
_____
_____
_____
_____
_____
_____
_____

DIRECTIONS:
_____
_____
_____
_____
_____
_____
_____
_____
_____
_____
_____
_____

RECIPE:

92

INGREDIENTS:
_____
_____
_____
_____
_____
_____
_____
_____
_____
_____
_____
_____

DIRECTIONS:
_____
_____
_____
_____
_____
_____
_____
_____
_____
_____
_____
_____
_____
_____

DIFFICULTY:
☐☐☐☐☐

RATING:
♡♡♡♡♡

SERVES:
....

COOKING TEMP:
....

PREP TIME:
....

COOK TIME:
....

TOOLS:
....
....
....
....
....
....

93

RECIPE:

DIFFICULTY:
☐ ☐ ☐ ☐ ☐

RATING:
♡ ♡ ♡ ♡ ♡

SERVES:
....

COOKING TEMP:
....

PREP TIME:
....

COOK TIME:
....

TOOLS:
....
....
....
....
....

INGREDIENTS:

DIRECTIONS:

RECIPE:

94

INGREDIENTS:

DIRECTIONS:

DIFFICULTY:
☐☐☐☐☐

RATING:
♡♡♡♡♡

SERVES:

COOKING TEMP:

PREP TIME:

COOK TIME:

TOOLS:

95

RECIPE:

DIFFICULTY:
☐☐☐☐☐

RATING:
♡♡♡♡♡

SERVES:

COOKING TEMP:

PREP TIME:

COOK TIME:

TOOLS:

INGREDIENTS:

DIRECTIONS:

RECIPE:

96

INGREDIENTS:

_____
_____
_____
_____
_____
_____
_____
_____
_____
_____
_____
_____

DIRECTIONS:

_____
_____
_____
_____
_____
_____
_____
_____
_____
_____
_____
_____
_____
_____
_____
_____

DIFFICULTY:
☐☐☐☐☐

RATING:
♡♡♡♡♡

SERVES:
....

COOKING TEMP:
....

PREP TIME:
....

COOK TIME:
....

TOOLS:
....
....
....
....
....
....

97

RECIPE:

DIFFICULTY:
☐☐☐☐☐

RATING:
♡♡♡♡♡

SERVES:

COOKING TEMP:

PREP TIME:

COOK TIME:

TOOLS:

INGREDIENTS:

DIRECTIONS:

RECIPE:

98

INGREDIENTS:

DIFFICULTY:
☐☐☐☐☐

RATING:
♡♡♡♡♡

SERVES:
....

COOKING TEMP:
....

DIRECTIONS:

PREP TIME:
....

COOK TIME:
....

TOOLS:
....
....
....
....
....
....

99

RECIPE:

DIFFICULTY:
☐☐☐☐☐

RATING:
♡♡♡♡♡

SERVES:

COOKING TEMP:

PREP TIME:

COOK TIME:

TOOLS:

INGREDIENTS:

DIRECTIONS:

RECIPE:

100

INGREDIENTS:

DIFFICULTY:

RATING:
♡♡♡♡♡

SERVES:

COOKING TEMP:

DIRECTIONS:

PREP TIME:

COOK TIME:

TOOLS:

Printed in Great Britain
by Amazon